THE OLD PHILOSOPHER

VI KHI NAO

THE OLD PHILOSOPHER

NIGHTBOAT BOOKS
NEW YORK

ISBN 978-1-937658-48-9

Design and typesetting by Margaret Tedesco
Text set in Myriad and Sabon
Cover art by Leslie Lerner: *A Scout Under A Copper Sky*, 2000
Acrylic on mounted canvas
Courtesy of Jill Lerner

Cataloging-in-publication data is available
from the Library of Congress

Nightboat Books
New York
www.nightboat.org

for Ruth & Tania

CONTENTS

dear god i am god

the angels fold their wings a flock of them

which means god   is clapping

dear god i am god

i ~~am~~ am washing myself in dew

transgender performance art as identity

FOG

the sun drops his knee on fog

a diurnal genuflection that

explains the lack of clarity in the prayer's thought

when god prays to himself

using the fog's opaque cushion

we know god is a child

who pretends to pray

because in the midst of his holy make-believe childhood

he is a beautiful version of daffodil twirling in dew

AA MEETING FOR A LIMESTONE

Today is my last day.

My lipless lips can't talk a river no more.

About being drunk sitting by the river.

Almost toppled over by another human-sized stone.

They are going to cut me into slats.

And they are going to edge my pretty face

In pure acid and grind my face down into

Dust and ash and draw lines and blots and squeeze

My face beneath a metal rod with macerated paper

Until I beseech the gods for mercy.

This is like a preventative AA meeting

So that I can talk shit about my pain, delirium, my lack

Of total control, my torture before it all happens.

Like preventive mastectomy for my emotional soul.

So it doesn't grow tumorous & obese.

See ya around, pancake faces.

BIRD POEM

I tell you the stars are moving lightly

& the birds are flapping in fright

They float aimlessly in the ether

Winter in their Heart

Summer in their Thyroid Gland

Spring in their Liver

Fall in their Left Temple

You stir stones in the pot made of iron—

You stir the seeds of civilization in light & in water—

Love is light, you say

For lunch, we eat pebbles

The small stones fall down our esophagus

And sink down the ravine of our stomach

Butterflies on our chest.

Life outside of the thyroid gland

The birds are strung to the pebbles

Down near our diaphragm

Like paperweights glued to a balloon

We are sore from living life & from making love day & night

What kind of love is this

When it can be broken in segments inside our diaphragm

Ready to burst into ravenous flight on its way out of our mouths?

HOW CAN SOMETHING SO UNMOVING
MOVE EVERYTHING AROUND IT

The heart is a quiet mountain in the Northern Hemisphere of the Body.

Darkness falls, but the heart lies still.

Others say the heart dies and then is reborn.

Jeremiah says, *The heart is deceitful*

Above all things, and desperately wicked.

The mountain does not have eyes or mouths

So how can it direct the shadows of Lucifer

Through the landscape of its own erosion?

Some say the mountain is made of glass.

Born as earth and rock, the glass mountain

Does not shatter.

And some say the heart is cold like a large stone.

But how can something so unmoving

Move everything around it?

There are different names for the heart:

Mount Hood, for instance, which lies

In Oregon like an alligator.

THE OLD PHILOSOPHER

Three cars pull down the cul-de-sac

& approximately four thousand

Two hundred and forty-five

Birds fly from

The trunks' wide mouths

One still remains inside

Walking back and forth on the gray carpet

With wings behind its back

Like an old philosopher

Socrates perhaps

Meanwhile

A drop of rain sits down

To pray

THE DAY GOD SMOKES MY GRANDMOTHER

God pulls my grandmother

Out of a finely made cigarette pack

Made of human tobacco & Long Khanh's red earth &

Bed sheets as long

As a rubber tree.

My family—all twenty of us—my grandmother,

My cousins, my aunts and uncles

All lie in a large cigarette cot

Called a bed with tinfoil bed sheets pulled to our chins.

We lie in rows on top of each other.

Over soft bones.

While my uncle steps out into my grandmother's grapevine.

He withdraws a cigarette from

His jean pocket and drags a smoke.

A cigarette smoking a cigarette.

Meanwhile, God pulls my grandmother

Out of her cigarette bed.

She is wedged between my first aunt and my second aunt.

He thumps her head against the wooden lid of the well &

Lights my grandmother's head up.

A fluttering of smoke is steamed out of her toes.

God inhales and exhales the soul of my grandmother

Until she withers and becomes an accordion of ash.

Then God flicks the rest of my grandmother across

Our neighbor's spinach garden.

God and my uncle take turns smoking.

While God finishes nearly a pack of us—one by one—

My uncle still ponders over his last three,

Sitting in their nearly empty compartment.

My uncle stares into the ashtray of his hand

And sobs until his hand becomes soot.

We stay inside of our floorboard cigarette case

And ponder when God is going to

Develop lung cancer

From smoking us.

Not long ago, in Long Khanh,

God handrolls his own cigarettes.

God licks the sides of our bed sheets

With his wet tongue.

And rolls me into a thin tobacco-burrito.

God smokes my cousin first, the one who was run over by a train

In my uncle's backyard, near my grandmother's grapevine.

God, the chronic smoker, likes his cigarettes

Aged three.

Short and stumpy.

God doesn't like to smoke me.

I smell too much like a conflicting

Mixture of lavender and walleye.

MY FIRST LOVER SAID I HAD A SMALL TONGUE

my first lover said i had a small tongue & it was hard to

french kiss me. that there were three disks on my body

that were softer than paper pesos. that i loved sour sour

sour sour sour food. unripe guavas & the essence. or

that you knew your voice would conquer the world. or

you knew something in you that was conquerable? that

there was conquest & spain & cadiz & the strait of g. not g-spot,

mind you. africa. or that you knew there was no afterlife & that i

knew the meaning of life & i held the

clave to the universe? that there were a thousand minds

unwinding in the distance & the ozone layer is climbing

the stairs from babylon. or that you could speak

vietnamese if you to wanted & if i wanted to. or that the tongue

was like a hammock, rocking the mouth in the

heat, dividing the atmosphere & hemisphere. & there

was snow between us. or that you knew there were no windows

into souls & there was no such thing as clave &

clave & clave or that there was a lighthouse in the

moon's backyard. that the world did not spin but spent its days sitting in walmart's toilet? or that you knew i knew that love was made of dust & light & maybe nails where the hammer walked away & then returned. or that you knew that spring was drying its wet fingers on the sleeves of winter's polar coat & that the snail was crawling slowly from my memory & sitting quietly on the throne of your memory. or my memory was your memory & that the tongue had no infrastructure & electricity was the lymphatic drainage?

BIBLICAL FLESH

What is torture ?   In the 2nd millennium BC   But the fiber   of knowing

that your lover's heart is made   of thorn?   Your tongue   soft,

flaming   like   the   desert   you have not   asked   her to be   unfaithful

but what about   the widening of   the   tripod   muscles   and   the camera   legs

When your   lover   screams into ecstasy   with   another?   Is it   will   or is

it Mary Magdalene   wailing away in your pillowcase?   As if you have

been dug out   of Canaan   to be completely   destroyed by your hand in

Someone else's sleeve   and   what the fuck do you know about   borrowed thorn

and the burning   bush   hidden   inside   your Cunt Book of Exodus ?   Is it

love?   Is it clarity?   Is it narrative? that allows   you to drag

your lover's   Masoretic flesh out of Egypt   into   Canaan? Thieves of manuscript

Thieves of paradise   sexual details   of   milk & honey   while you hold

your   staff   of contemporary hallucinogenic   interpretation and thrust it into   coeval wasteland   that never forgets to   moan   or sigh or murmur

your   hidden Hebrew name   And you   stand still in your delayed prophesied

pleasure   and ask   the obvious: by the staff,   is it you who gets

fucked or   is it   God? You   lean   gently in   the esoteric breeze

beneath a   dogwood tree   while   with Moses' blind   vision inside you   your

2nd lover licks   the salt off   the one-page bible   concealed in between your

peripheral thighs   You   think it's scholarly your lover eating you   page

by page   her tongue turning   paper cut   blood leading you out of the torture

well   water high above the waist   and the desert   is so far

carrying a mirage you   memorized, an image   of you   bitching and wailing,

west of the Jordan River oh biblical flesh biblical flesh You unclench your fist &

brush your lover's long hair back   into the forbidden breeze while droplets of

tears , salty not from pleasure but from   emotional torture,   deplane your

face like   small   waterbed   volcanoesbefore erupting Later you walk   slowly   near the ants on the yellow grass made of   1st millennium BC &

measure the long   glances   of time   above your head   when the grass will

be as tall as you   and hide your body   as if it were a forgotten

sexual facility   The ants   crawl away carrying a weight three times their strength

and you lift your   leather   sandal as if to crush just a footstep away   Your toes shake

their heads like guests   at a one-star hotel   You book one night in the Promised Land

of the Israelites and wait   for your 3rd lover to arrive   and read you back

the torturous verses   concealed in packages of salt inside you   Then you turn

to Lot's wife and ask,   "Was   the view worth it? Is it   still gorgeous?"

HAY BALE & ASPHALT

The woman with hay bale   of

Hair exited the public

Toilet walking slowly, dragging a confetti of cornfield with her   head

She is grass, legume, fodder drifting beneath the field   of

                                                        gametes

The man is a mixture   of

                                                  bituminous

Pitch with sand or gravel & why chromosome?

Some say it was an event of a sleeping policeman

Hay bale   non asphalt

She sped out on his speed   bump

CLEAN LIKE A PLATE

leaves of November   rotate her shoulders

while a naked baby is walking alone in the middle of the

highway without geometric snowboots   her hair

a whisper   of retired shadow

there is no transparency in this

just the vocal cord of daylight stuffed to the brim with

human   discontinuity   &

neonatal sauntering

the child walks an ontological walk   one

foot of melancholy   over

one foot of bliss

some say this is a nascent gesture of the dismal the father

comes crawling out of the wilderness like a smile

destroyed   in the   face of resentment   the

mother   an   obtuse   triangle   not like a highway

warning sign   not like an indecision

        after giving birth   as her geometrical figure indicates

                                                she is not a stop sign

for the child   to stop walking   in the nude   she is not going

to be a trapezoid

any time   soon   the child is clean like a plate

                    of dessert   Nature   strays   in

            the moment   &   a state patrol officer

in his patrol car   stops & asks the child:

do you need a ride?

no, thank you, officer   the child replies   but if you don't mind

picking up   after my diaper i left stumped in Yorkshire

that would be   wonderful i don't want the winter birds heading

 explosively south to beak & admire chocolate

                                                while choking

                                                on elasticity

IN THE DIURNAL BATH

in the diurnal bath   we sit   rubbing

inhospitable splendor onto our eyelids   here we can access a roomful of heartaches

boxes of melancholia &   sweet basil   stacked tall

we retrieve them by mourning into a

                                forklift   lodged vagrantly

in our subconscious   we caress

the edge of misery

                        floating into an evening

of stardom

our heart holds   its pulsing

purple
                        dress

                        by the collar

heartbeats do not count   how many lives they have led

they die as soon   as

                        they are born

TODAY I LOST MY HAT

Today I lost my hat, took the wrong bus to work,
grandmother died.

And the panic voiced in my mother's esophagus.

Before Dawn: A funeral landed at my door. Inside. The
roof of my mouth imploding with muttering liquid. The
rain poured down. The fingers of rain droplets digging
into my skin. Fog hovered over the earth like a giant
shroud.

Morning: I hung my wet sock on the giant coffee maker. A
co-worker offered his large winter glove as a makeshift
sock. In two hours, the warm breath evaporating out of the
throat of the sock steamed my toes.

Brunch: When the sun did not show up for work. When there was much dying to do.

Lunch: Rice tasted like raw goat milk. This afternoon. The sun did not burn.

Evening: The moon dancing, tumbling off the precipice of the universe. Did Lucifer know that she couldn't be touched? Even when she was decadent, mellowed, indecisive? Even when she fell into the lap of Eden, her white globular head tossing in the wind of stars, her face pressing into the bosom of yesterday's dream?

How death makes one suffer!

PASTORAL THRESHOLD

I knew she wasn't capable of loving me back. I knew
this even before she knew it herself. Yet, I continued
to pursue her, giving her those feverish side-glances
between the ivy vines that only a man in love is
capable of giving a woman. I knew this long before I
was born and long before olive oil was poured on
my head and made me a slave to my own God. She
had been grieving on and off, going through bouts of
insomnia, tossing vicodin and aspirin down her
throat for a small infection below the left knee, but I
knew better, I knew she had been under the grand
impression that the medications were codependent
agents she was abusing in order to cope with her
husband's sudden extinction, that delicious husband
of hers, the one I sent to Syria as a UN inspector.
I knew Syria was housing chemical weapons and
I knew there were snipers and I knew that in his
search for their existence and their recent application
he would die soon after I sent him there. I was told

through my own personal informant that it was the speediest way to get someone killed. Days after his death or rather his assassination, she was squirming in my arms, under the opulent bed sheets of the Emirates Palace in Abu Dhabi where I housed my lust. I was deep inside her, my newly-wedded wife, while her eyes were closed and I was staring straight up into the glass fortress of the crystal chandelier above our heads and I knew it wouldn't be long before the crown sitting on my head would be turned into a seat cushion for some bastard's sovereign asshole. In the middle of the night, long before I withdrew my monarchical foreskin from her pastoral threshold, my iPhone lit up. Nathan texted me and told me he would be expecting me at the Hakkasan Restaurant at 8 a.m. military time. He cc'd God and of course, her dead husband, Uriah. I didn't even know the dead owned phones! In the hotel shower, I told myself, "David! David! You planned this the worst way possible. You bastard you."

DESPOTIC HUSH

I have this fantasy, in the open meadow, of baking
my virgin body open for her in the winter
strawberries, berries so red, floating meekly,
nakedly, feasting on snow. She is standing at the
great crossing, her eyeslonging, aching in the
distance, gazing far into the dark flesh of the musky,
desolate night. Her flesh. To fill me. So velvety blue.
Her blouse filled with blue mead and prairie.
Standing there in suspended despair. Such is the
first half of the 20th century of her body. Her skirt
heats Ur like an oven. Much later, on a less
controversial evening, she is on her Euphratic knees,
sucking my clitoris dry like the bone of the small,
desiccated deluge. Not long ago, inside the Elohist
source, my arms around her waist, the genealogy of
desire traces its fingers, its lineage pre-heated
around my clavicle, a necklace of wild purrs and
rivets roaring for God, while I hold her form tightly

around my body. Was her kiss primeval? Or was my
longing impartial? I complicate our cycle of dispute,
her Canaan and my Canaan, with despotic hush
and rush. Forward backward a little bit in time,
when her face is buried in my neck, Jacob's tongue
undulating on his barren mother's bare chest, I
suffuse the history of Babylonian exile by closing my
eyes and closing her eyes. If I had to hold something
in captivity, why not her revulsion for dirty fat
wrapped in loincloth, feeble gold, and rasping rain?
Had I resented the raw meat of human life? The
thick temple of her desertion? She and I, our flesh
tight in the prairie. When I lift the golden blouse
above her head and set our timer for disarray, and
she is sympatric and beautiful, and I am naked,
raspy, soft and rustic above her, rubbing in inertia,
in motion, in baking sheet, in redwheelbarrow our
eager meat tight, white, a knot, of sedimentary

fucking, the victuals, of kernel, core, nucleus, the

nub and gist of my tight muscles clutching her

swollen inner thighs, and the animal flesh of her

sucking on my neck, on my tongue, on my nipples,

on my thighs, these divisions of want and the harsh,

guttural depth of my moaning and so quiet the grass

beneath the solid, muscle-bound weight of her

thrusting up into me so that when yeast unites with

salt and sugar and the construction of hand on top

of hand, arms wrapping pussy to pussy, fingers

interlaced hers and mine, and of my arching back

bent like an eel into a crescent the descending

stratosphere of flour-woken clouds that arouse the

Euphrates river to speak to swine and exiles while

the hour's heat bakes the earth and the dormant

culture inside me seized by a geopolitical orgasm

makes the second bell toll, shaking its metallic skirt

like a timer once again as she widens her circle of

ecstasy. It seems all instrumental, afterward, the way
our desire expands on the wet grass as our bodies
shake, and I am in her arms and I am inside her,
breasts overlapping breasts like post-kneaded dough
over post-kneaded dough, I think how seamless the
flesh is when it wants to amalgamate and how such
a plant with long narrow leaves, wild and tireless
and flattened, is so capable of offering post-
pomegranatic and post-pastry pleasure relinquished
by Demeter's daughter to a few fear-driven souls
sitting in a semi-semiotic pitcher of sorrow. When
the night drops its monolithic elevation and she is
pouring her tongue into my mouth, I think, gee,
golly, how can we make this last, and how much I
love baking on grass.

A CUBAN BAY of PIGS

When I first met her, her face was hollowed out, like
a soggy tree carved from the center with a metal
spoon. I had asked them to do this to her because
she had the face of history and to me, it seemed, to
get rid of her face was to get rid of history. Each of
my countrymen expressed their devotion to me
differently, but she was an exception. She was a
political farce, and had the face of history, but she
also had the face of betrayal. She had exquisite,
poignant cheeks, pink and pointed and round and
they indicated simply to me that she would sell me
out. Her cheekbones had given this aspect of her
character away. Even Judas Iscariot, the apostle,
couldn't blow kisses at her. But now, she is black like
nightmare. Now, she is in front of me, faceless and
deteriorating. Her entire head is soaked with
plaster. In the wind, the dried-out plaster from the
edges of her face will blow like tattered white glass.

I ordered the officers to fill her head with packages of bubble gum, snicker bars, and skittles. Her face is a piñata to be hung from a tree. I have ordered the children to come out of school a couple of hours earlier and my officers are going to escort them one child at a time toward a mulberry tree, where young boys and young girls with bats in their hands prepare to earn their treats and sweets. My friend, Fidel Castro, taught me how to celebrate. She spent most of her life in a headdress and I couldn't understand why women need a face to begin with. From her, I learned the art of substitution, which is also the art of omission. I have learned to celebrate women like a Cuban Bay of Pigs. Take a woman's face away and you have taken everything from her. Today is a great day to embrace her deformity. Let me take you to the children and ask them what their favorite candies are.

NYMPHAEA CAERULEA

It was in the Ibrahimia District that I caught her
smile like a lid on a pot. The steam bitches the seam
of the pot and the lid together, providing me a false
glance of the collective terror to come. However, it
was my poor eyesight that allowed me to mistake
the tear gas for the steam that fluttered like her
gelatinous scarf beneath the muffler in late
winter. It was an ardent task loving her. I had taken
sneak previews in between the peripheral partitions
of the riot-rage landscape. The dark clouds above.
The bomb squads. Inhaling her and then inhaling
the tear gas. I dropped and coughed even though
my eyes did all the coughing or rather dripping. I
dropped and dripped and she did the same through
the other wall where the red sea of blown and
injured bodies and torches separated her dementia
from my dementia. I wheeled my arthritic legs at a
98 degree angle as if they were a chariot that Ben
Hur rode, and picked up the brisk pace of .000276

kilometers per hour towards her. I carted my
nonagenarian body as if it were a hot tea pot ready
to spill over and with my nonagenarian muscles,
curled a senescent bouquet of *Nymphaea caerulea*
donned in Latin and in a lachrymatory shroud
around my shaking fingers; I couldn't tell if it was
an effect of my trembling heart or Parkinson's. I
didn't know by then how pushing the corridor of
my neophytic desire through the threshold of
walking and falling toward a blurry landscape also
known as my beloved would make my blood wobble
like so. Bent over like a low-lit lamp shade, I made
tiny swaying shuffles like tiny ambient leaf music
and found from the peripheral views, the sketchy
incandescent and evanescent topography of my
newly-planted love stretched out on a tarmac floor.
Her dark nonagenarian skin on her face and hands
coated under the debris of ash was an epochal
croissant flaked with dark powdered sugar. It might

take hours or even days to unlock centimeters off the ashy dress-rehearsal-of-war filming her entire breathing soul. I rushed quickly to her side at .0023 kilometers per hour, my heart in tremor. Then it occurred to me, and it is perhaps impossible to tell if it was fleece, tear gas, wool or hair or amnesia or misdirection that created a veneer of doubt over my forehead and tongue and compelled me to see and taste that I had rushed too quickly and too oversightedly to a tarp that blanketed the wreckage which I mistook for a nonagenarian woman!

YOU CALLED YOURSELF JOSHUA

You asked me once where I buried the snow. Along
the river or was it along the spine of your brother's
childhood as he stood rigidly before the tall pine. I
clapped the darkness with a walnut stick as the
applause emerged from your mouth through the
opaque window, which you mistook for a foggy
Saturday. You write on my body with fresh walnut
husk, the rich oilseed hiding inside you, and while it's
fresh and verdant, I wait for you to oxidize. It's
the skin that writes, you say tadpolely. You called
yourself Joshua. You called yourself Joshua. But I
thought love was an act of chemical analysis. A
place to measure your zinc to fatty acids production
ratio. Was it too much to ask? On the first date? On
the second? While you buried your smell like I
buried snow—as if yesterday couldn't stand to be by
itself. I woke you up along a bank to tell you that a
phallusless lion just made love to me and you had

no choice but to watch. My back arched. To write
on my skin, you transported yourself through
different centuries, and asked in that dream, did you
want to watch or be watched? You clawed me and
then you called yourself Joshua. You clawed my
shirt off in the middle of the night and called
yourself Joshua. Post-oxidation, whatever you wrote
on my body became black. As if to write, to truly
write, is to fuck darkness. And you love fucking
darkness, don't you, I privately ask? I love telling the
truth, you say. You close my eyes with your mouth
and my eyelids become *falling cherry blossoms*. I love
darkness more than I love light. I love you when
you oxidize. I love this and nothing more.

AS SOON AS

There are days when

As soon as

The night rolls her

Eyes back into herself

As if experiencing orgasm

In silhouetted solitude

I lick the lazy door

And stand in the corridor, waiting

While she makes me feel that

I am on the brink of drinking poison

Prisms, nocturnal lights bouncing

Off a panther's undulating

Back.

CHORUS OF BUTTONS

Get blindfolded by refrains

Of ochre threads over blue

In sight, slits made for beauty

For labor to garment the skin

While 'unlocking the air' for

A gentle Velvet Revolution

The blazer is a sartorial ballad

Of uniformity for land-based

Outings such as a Czechoslovakian

Protest or crickets picnicking on a boat

The slack is a pair of silos yarned out of sheep skin

To preserve crops, enthusiasm, or missiles

Or, to unzip, for demonstration

Whole grains tumble out like weeds in the wind

The shirt is a monopoly of warmth

Even its ambassador, the collar

Has to re-stitch its political beliefs

To match the parliamentary pantyhose

MY SOCIALIST SALIVA

My seven-year-old face pressed onto the serene field of my mother's back

As she rode her motorcycle through the red earth

Flanked by rubber trees

With arboreal nipples pouring out   alabaster

Blood cells—its viscidity meant to

Pipe out the clothesline

      that hung my breath

      while trying to fold my saliva into a socialist shirt

After the sun had dried out my mouth

And my face   not a place for blood transfusions

I held my mouth open

To receive the aromatic rain of rambutan & coffee beans

The wind tossing   &   turning as my mother circulated us around a curve

My mother's hair flipping through the pages of the air

The rubber trees   tall and skinny

Whose backs wouldn't break very easily

My mother rode me on land coated with   rambutans

Rambutans were like little ball hearts growing red hair

The earth of Long Khanh was swollen with such cardiovascular beauties

My little heart was a little engine

Of red earth—the streets of my childhood were walking to & fro

There were times though when the Viet Cong

Came through my grandmother's grapevine

And took my mother's sewing machines, measuring tapes

Fabrics from China of indefinite lengths

While I emerged from under, after tucking myself away on the tongue of a banana leaf

Near the coconut tree in my grandmother's backyard

When the flood came—it puked out pig's intestinal debris, needles & threads,
    oxtails, hair

As if the earth were a seamstress, crumpling the áo bà ba of regression

For rain to arrive at the threshold of its sleeve as pluvial tyranny

Once in a while a child fell through a well

And another child or two drowned in a swimming pool

My grandmother's body, a helicopter

                                        ran through her in Saigon

Its heliocentric blades cutting her skin & bleeding crimson fence wires

That demarcated the pastoral field of her elbow from the suburb of her bicep

My Uncle Binh—he came dashing through my grandmother's grapevine

Toward my mother's seamstress business

With big plastic bags—he came through—throttling my mother's in-progress
    áo dài

Feminine, scissors, thread—anything he could retrieve with his bare hands

While pulling the earth of my mother's labor

Through the corridor of someone else's ruins

The Viet Cong couldn't come after him—after all—they were busy

Confiscating my mother's extensive assembly line of sewing machines

When I came back to Long Khanh

Over eleven months ago—in the aching month of January

My Uncle Binh turned to me while my eyes searched for Nadal

On screen and told me

He once accidentally burned me with a cigar butt

He said if I ever get depressed in the States and want a different kind
    of oppression

Call him and he would buy me a ticket home

And we could inhale oyster shells together under a blanket made of
intestinal veins

A blanket the communists would stitch with the needle of their greed

I suppose I could go on

UNTITLED

My mother is a shadow

That a centipede climbs over

To find its home

THE ARBOREAL MUSEUM

There stand the trees at the end of the world where the leaves have been painted by Rothko, Monet, Cassatt, Kahlo, Nerdrum each in their own style. It is a museum curated by humanity and nature. Open your eyes and sit beneath the trees and eat your apples. Let the paint rain upon you, droplets of resin, pigment, solvent, perfume of iridescence.

REDOLENT HOMOSEXUALITY

the bicycle seat is sitting on the pink table as a nose

sniffling a pink notepad.

blue ink. purple calculator:

the difficulty lies in rivets.

not in life. not in digits.

a man is giving instructions on how to remove derivatives

from a horse

is the horse flamboyant, a homosexual?

you rise from the counter

and you ask the groom if you can drive by sniffling at it.

gaudy contours, human confetti,

condoms stretched over the saddle

a wedding cake

you propose a toast:

to the marriage that thrives on an odor.

ONE RIB REMOVED

Almost—This fallen

Biblical step—almost removes me

From the timeline of grasping

This fallen step—almost a remorse drawn

Into impulse

Traps my cranium in bones—in flesh

My memory inspired by

The panting imbued by sound—of the import-

Ance of ritual—of the habit

Deleting—that

Missing note from the lungs—cripples my

Breath Timekeeper

Takes metonymic note—

This at that time—

I my ribs are piano keys

The piano grasps for my body Falling—But later

When a key a rib is

Removed from me—

My breath   skips a note

My breath   skips a breath

My breath   skips a step on the stairs of breathing—

Whisper, murmur, collapse:

Annihilate the odor of naming

Altering the chronometer garden

Inside my cranium—

The Human Male

THE ENIGMATIC DEMOISELLE, *ELOIGN*

A crowd gathers at the opening paragraph

A crowd of words

Afraid to look at other words

For what they might see

The 't' in 'tenuous' is excited about the 't' in 'tampion'

We are wearing matching shoes

Words are fearful of their origins

One word will condemn another word

Or annihilate another completely

Lynch that man

That brisk fascist

Or remove that vixen

She doesn't belong in our elite

Class of linguistic nobility

Words gather and group themselves into families

Ones that share similar symmetries

Or think they would like to bring another member

One especially that doesn't belong here

Let me introduce you to the enigmatic demoiselle, *Eloign*

Please say hello. Welcome. Welcome

Social pressures and semantic infrastructure prevent words

From being individuals

Why can't I stay alone in an empty room?

Floating from one blank page into another

Some words are deliberately weak

Join a club. Being a member of many things

Happy to find themselves appearing in a maxim

Right here I won't become extinct

Or disappear into the past

Or get snatched away like a child in front of a bus stop

Words refuse to elucidate

Their clans of urgent meaning

After they kiss each other goodbye—

They disperse into a field of nonsense

Or into a cliché

Many words enter a queue

Collaborate with one another

To form an allegiance

Of melancholy

Many exist in nomadic tribes

                Called The Sentences
                Many prefer to live in a fragment

Refusing to tame their unruly insinuations

A few words remain sentient in a mansion

Gazing down at imposing height

At their aristocratic isolation

But before the god of elocution—

Words are merely nudes

In their veneer sense of homelessness

SNOW

When God superimposes his imagination on my primal flesh

He casts a shadow that looks like wine

If I have been good, God

Superimposes the soul of an

Angel onto my primal

Flesh + it casts a shadow

That looks like snow

WINE SLEEPS

in its blood

red casket

with its

fermented

eyes closed

SKYSCRAPER

1

The mind of the seamstress is so free to curb, as it breaks through the inner cell, the vast circular silence of memory. She opens her memories into snow banks. The curtain of pores. Memories are absconding and there is no one to house its current resident. The body is glad that a part of its body remembers. The birth of its death. It stays indoors. The pores and their interior closets of blood vessels are watching the rain. They are watching and waiting. Watching their activities outside of their front doors.

2

The skin is a skyscraper with many windows. Window washing. Not with Windex. Guava scented soap. They watch the soapy sea foams fall past the pores. The blood vessels gaze through the curtains of water and skin. The pores are excited about the limelight. Excited about the dove and the guava and the soap and the summer in their appropriate hemisphere. The rain comes and washes their heartbeats away. The rain comes and becomes so great with height and light. The rain and one blood vessel in the cubicle of pores gaze out of the window and wonder if they should run out and live or commit suicide.

3

One drop of blood stands still against time and wanders through the house of the hemoglobin, the different empty rooms of the body. They question. They have a lot of questions. What are they doing inside the surface of skin? The blood floats and the blood floats. The blood sprints and spirals (slow and steady) along the endless racetrack of the blood tunnel. Watching activities and life from the inside and gazing out of their red tinted windows and not being able to stop a thing from proceeding (dead or alive, animate or inanimate). The blood, after all, is not hired by the body to be the sentry. A needle enters the bloodstream. It will move along this river until its intellectual eye pierces one caliginous island along the Pacific Ocean. The kidney or liver? Perhaps the lucrative needle desires to move upstream to drill through a fleshier, more copious thing called the heart. Soft, veiny boulders. There. There. An oil spill.

4

The mind of the seamstress, for the moment, suspends before opening its lips from the mountain top. The top container of the body. The top layer in a bento box. Other people are becoming less of themselves. The mind is afraid to dine with despair. It has become a fantastic kisser of the side of the door.

5

After the needle drops into her blood stream, the woman cries. The needle is poking at death, prickling its blood in a pool of blood. Her tears are tears, of course. But what's most important is that they are interlocking tears. No one can enter; not even a quiet smile.

6

Your kind is unbelievably soft like the doorway into eternity, says the needle as it enters the flesh portal of the heart. The seamstress is expecting this. Everywhere is a door. A pinch alerts and lets her know that there won't be operatic rehearsals in the atria. Death does not rehearse. All kings are afraid of their own birthday, says the needle to the seamstress. Now that you are dying, you are becoming more conscious of morning glories. They bloom on the interior walls of your stomach like English ivies.

7

With a rifle, an incorrigible boy of 17 years of age enters a family-owned convenience store and requests the owner to hand over all the cash. When the owner pushes his son behind him, the robber mistakes it as a sign of alerting the cops of the robbery and shoots the owner in the head twice. The criminal remembers the startled eyes of the son as he reaches over the cash register for the cash.

8

Before she dies, the seamstress remembers. She remembers because the bedroom floor of her mind is climbing the interior walls of her English-ivied stomach. Before she dies, she craves guava juice that floats freely on bento boxes. What if the Atlantic Ocean was segmented and compartmentalized into bento boxes. On the off chance that there is an oil spill, the humans can quarantine and substitute it for another. To be emptied and cleaned and refilled with salt water, the appropriate kind of cuttlefish, the right family of minnows. It will sit near the windowsill, practicing its water-curling techniques. Out of its familiar environment, a wave won't neglect its art form.

9

The body nominates the kidney to purify the blood. But perhaps the vocation belongs to every body part. Everyone must participate. Only the elbows do not care, largely ignored until injury.

10

There is no guava juice on the table, on the kitchen counter, or in the refrigerator. The seamstress is aware of this. Before she dies, one part of her body will sample the scent of guava. On the body of a brand new soap. The seamstress climbs into her stone shower stall and turns one spigot left and the other right.

11

It's raining. The blood does not need to dive 150 feet out from the pores to commit suicide. The blood does not need to roam. The conscientious body does all the menial work for all the employees it hires. Including immediate termination without proper evaluations. No more monthly reviews. No more files hidden in the epidermis.

12

While the rain washes the windows, the sky-
scraper collapses. For 2 hours and 20 minutes
the pores drink in the scent of a memory, a
portal between oblivion and permanence before
the ambulance comes. In the binary world, in
the world without God, after a life of solid
exists a life of liquid. In the binary world, in the
world with God, rain and skyscraper take turns
wearing each other's clothes.

ACKNOWLEDGEMENTS

My gratitude for my magnanimous teachers: C.D.Wright, Forrest Gander, and Tipu Attar, who are my literary sister, mother, and father. They provide endless love, support, and guidance.

Poems in these pages have appeared in: *Elimae, VISION, Triggerfish Critical Review, Birkensnake, Forklift, Ohio, Reality Beach,* and *Academy of American Poets.*

The author wishes to thank Jill Lerner for the use of her husband's art.

Vi Khi Nao was born in Long Khanh, Vietnam. She holds an MFA in fiction from Brown University, where she received the John Hawkes and Feldman Prizes in fiction and the Kim Ann Arstark Memorial Awards in poetry. Her work includes poetry, fiction, film, and cross-genre collaboration. She is the author of two novellas, *Swans in Half-Mourning* and *The Vanishing Point of Desire*. Her novel, *Fish in Exile*, will make its first appearance in Fall 2016 from Coffee House Press.

NIGHTBOAT BOOKS

Nightboat Books, a nonprofit organization, seeks to develop audiences for writers whose work resists convention and transcends boundaries. We publish books rich with poignancy, intelligence, and risk. Please visit our website, www.nightboat.org, to learn about our titles and how you can support our future publications.

The following individuals have supported the publication of this book. We thank them for their generosity and commitment to the mission of Nightboat Books:

Elizabeth Motika
Benjamin Taylor

In addition, this book has been made possible, in part, by grants from the National Endowment for the Arts and the New York State Council on the Arts Literature Program.